UPDOG

US MILITARY BRANCHES

# THE US NAVY IN ACTION

Marie-Therese Miller

Lerner Publications ◆ Minneapolis

**To John, Harold, Warren, and all my family members and friends who bravely served in the US military. With heartfelt appreciation to all US Navy personnel.**



Lerner Publications Company
An imprint of Lerner Publishing Group, Inc.
241 First Avenue North
Minneapolis, MN 55401 USA

For reading levels and more information, look up this title at www.lernerbooks.com.

Main body text set in ITC Franklin Gothic Std.
Typeface provided by Adobe Systems.

**Designer:** Mary Ross
**Lerner team:** Sue Marquis

**Library of Congress Cataloging-in-Publication Data**

Names: Miller, Marie-Therese, author.
Title: The US Navy in action / Marie-Therese Miller.
Description: Minneapolis : Lerner Publications, [2023] | Series: US military branches (Updog Books) | Includes bibliographical references and index. | Audience: Ages 8–11 | Audience: Grades 4–6 | Summary: “Out on the sea, the navy works to keep the US safe. Discover how the navy formed during the Revolutionary War, its ships, the navy SEALs, and more”— Provided by publisher.
Identifiers: LCCN 2021043446 | ISBN 9781728458274 (library binding) | ISBN 9781728463582 (paperback) | ISBN 9781728462530 (ebook)
Subjects: LCSH: United States. Navy—Juvenile literature.
Classification: LCC VA58.4 .M55 2023 | DDC 359.00973—dc23

LC record available at https://lccn.loc.gov/2021043446

Manufactured in the United States of America
1-50856-50193-12/7/2021

# TABLE OF CONTENTS

# THE NAVY MISSION

Navy SEALs jump from a plane flying at 30,000 feet (9,144 m).

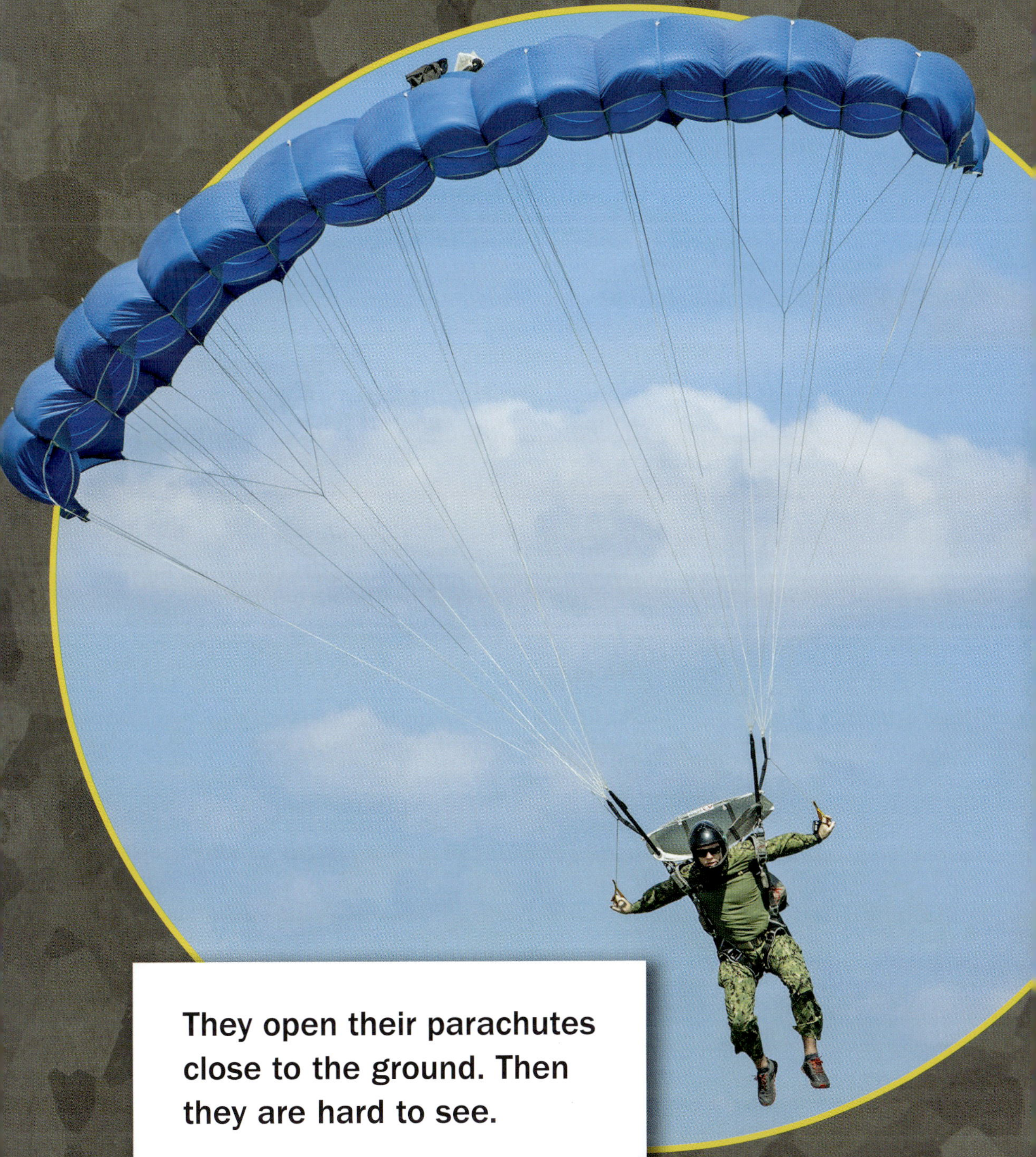

They open their parachutes close to the ground. Then they are hard to see.

The navy was formed in 1775.

It had a few ships during the Revolutionary War (1775–1783).

The navy's mission is to protect the US on the sea.

**MISSION:**
an important job or task

It also helps people in need, such as after a hurricane.

## UP NEXT!

**Carrying planes.**

# AIRCRAFT CARRIER LIFE

There are over seventy airfcraft on board the USS *Carl Vinson*.

**AIRCRAFT:**
a vehicle that travels through the air

The naval aircraft carrier has five thousand crew members.

# VEHICLE CLOSE-UP

**The CMV-22B Osprey has rotors that tilt. It takes off like a helicopter and flies like a plane.**

rotor
wing
wheels

Aircraft carriers are like small cities. The crew works day and night.

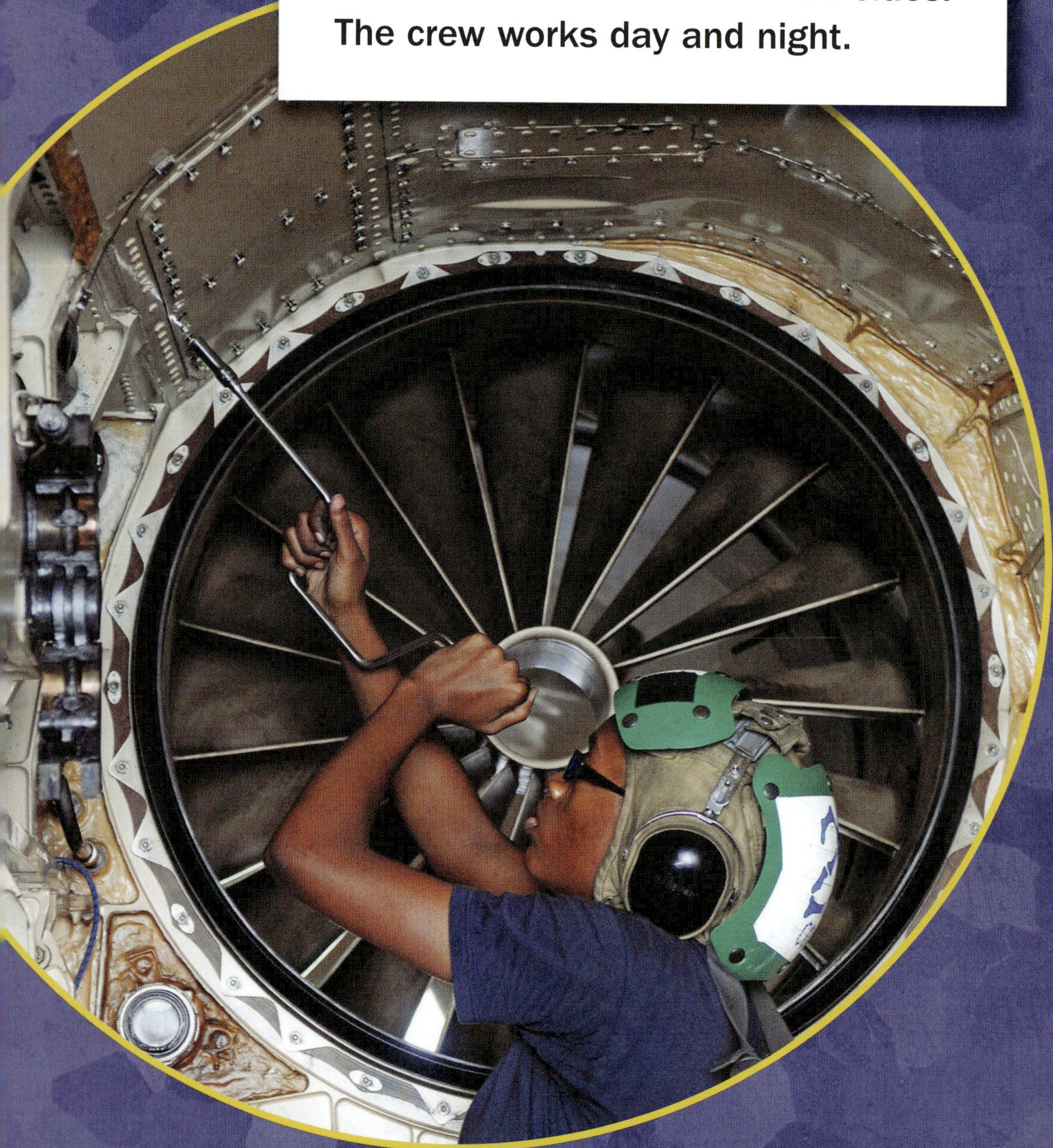

*Vinson* has two large mess decks, a post office, stores, and even a barbershop.

**MESS DECK:**
part of a ship where people eat, sleep, and relax

*Vinson* is longer than three football fields!

Planes launch from its flight deck.

# UP NEXT!

Navy aircraft.

# THE FLYING NAVY

F-35C Lightning II can travel at Mach 1.6.

**MACH:**
a way of measuring speed. Mach 1 is the speed of sound.

Radar has a hard time finding this plane.

The navy has about 450,000 people working to keep the United States safe.

# MILITARY MISSION

## THE NAVY HAS TO SNEAK IN TO SAVE SOMEONE FAR INLAND. WHAT'S THE BEST WAY?

A. A boat

B. A navy SEAL team to parachute in

C. An aircraft carrier

Answer: B

# GLOSSARY

**aircraft:** a vehicle that travels through the air

**Mach:** a way of measuring speed. Mach 1 is the speed of sound.

**mess deck:** part of a ship where people eat, sleep, and relax

**mission:** an important job or task

# CHECK IT OUT!


Abdo, Kenny. *United States Navy*. Minneapolis: Abdo Zoom, 2019.

Boothroyd, Jennifer. *Inside the US Navy*. Minneapolis: Lerner Publications, 2018.

Britannica Kids: Navy
https://kids.britannica.com/kids/article/navy/353522

Kiddle: United States Navy Facts for Kids
https://kids.kiddle.co/United_States_Navy

Kiddle: United States Navy SEALs Facts for Kids
https://kids.kiddle.co/United_States_Navy_SEALs

Morey, Allan. *U.S. Navy*. Minneapolis: Jump!, 2021.

# INDEX



# PHOTO ACKNOWLEDGMENTS

Image credits: U.S. Navy photo by Petty Officer 2nd Class Anthony Harding, p. 4; U.S. Air Force photo by Yasuo Osakabe, p. 5; NH KN-10855 courtesy of the Naval History & Heritage Command, pp. 6–7; U.S. Navy photo by Mass Communication Specialist Seaman Zachary S. Welch/flickr, p. 8; U.S. Navy photo by Mass Communication Specialist 2nd Class Kristopher Ruiz/flickr (CC BY 2.0), p. 9; U.S. Navy Photo by Mass Communication Specialist 3rd Class Eric Coffer/Wikimedia Commons, p. 10; U.S. Navy photo by Mass Communication Specialist Seaman Kristopher S. Haley/flickr, p. 11; U.S. Navy photo by Mass Communication Specialist 3rd Class Aaron T. Smith/United States Department of Defense, pp. 12–13; U.S. Navy photo by Mass Communication Specialist Seaman Apprentice Madailein Abbott/flickr, p. 14; U.S. Navy photo by Mass Communication Specialist Seaman Dartez C. Williams/flickr, p. 15; U.S. Navy Photo by Petty officer third class Protz/flickr, p. 16; U.S. Navy photo by Mass Communication Specialist 3rd Class Jasen/flickr (CC BY 2.0), p. 17; U.S. Navy photo by Chief Mass Communication Specialist Shannon E. Renfroe/flickr, p. 18; U.S. Navy photo by Mass Communication Specialist 3rd Class Kasey Krall/flickr, p. 19; U.S. Navy photo by Mass Communication Specialist 2nd Class Kaleb J. Sarten/flickr (CC BY 2.0), p. 20. Design elements: anyababii/Getty Images; Andrey_Kuzmin/Shutterstock.com; Andrey_Kuzmin/Shutterstock.com.

Cover: U.S. Navy photo by Mass Communication Specialist 3rd Class Joshua R. Warne/flickr.